SPORTS CARS

IAN GRAHAM

Heinemann Library
Chicago, Illinois

Customer Service 888-454-2279
Visit our website at www.heinemannlibrary.com

Designed by Jo Hinton-Malivoire and Tinstar Design Limited (www.tinstar.co.uk)
Illustrations by Geoff Ward
Originated by Dot Gradations Ltd
Printed and bound in Hong Kong, China, by South China Printing

07 06 05 04
10 9 8 7 6 5 4 3 2

Library of Congress Cataloging-in-Publication Data
Graham, Ian, 1953-
    Sports cars / Ian Graham.
       p. cm. -- (Designed for success)
    Summary: Provides an overview of the design and engineering
  of sports cars.
    Includes bibliographical references and index.
    ISBN 1-40340-772-X (Library binding-hardcover)
    1. Sports cars--Juvenile literature.   [1. Sports cars.]
I.Title. II. Series.
    TL236.G695 2003
    629.222'1--dc21
                        2002006120

Acknowledgments
The author and publishers are grateful to the following for permission to reproduce copyright material: pp. 1, 4, 5 (bottom), 21 (top), 28 Alvey and Towers; pp. 3, 6, 11 (bottom), 12, 13 (bottom), 20 (bottom), 21 (bottom), 25 (top) Car Photo Library/Dave Kimber; p. 5 (top) Auto Express/Phil Talbot; pp. 7 (bottom x 3), 13 (top), 15 (top and bottom), 16, 18, 22, 23 (top and bottom), 25 (bottom), 26, 27 (top), 29 Auto Express; p. 7 (top) Lotus; pp. 8, 9 (bottom) Eye Ubiquitous/Darren Maybury; pp. 9 (top), 24 (top) Corbis; p. 10 Eye Ubiquitous/Darren Maybury/McLaren; p. 11 (top) Colin Curwood; p. 14 McLaren; p. 17 (top) TRH Pictures; p. 19 (top) EPA; p. 24 (bottom) Eye Ubiquitous; p. 27 (bottom) Ariel Motor Company.

Cover photograph reproduced with permission of Car Photo Library.

Our thanks to David A. Garfield for his comments in the preparation of this book.

Every effort has been made to contact copyright holders of any material reproduced in this book. Any omissions will be rectified in subsequent printings if notice is given to the publishers.

Some words are shown in bold, **like this.** You can find out what they mean by looking in the glossary.

CONTENTS

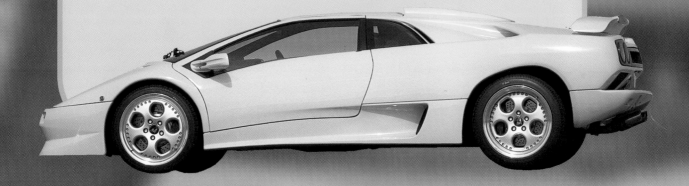

SPORTS CARS

A car's design reflects the way it will be used. Some cars are designed to carry a whole family and their luggage. Others are designed for making short trips on busy city streets. Sports cars are high-**performance** cars that are designed to be fun to drive.

Most sports cars are designed as high-performance road cars with high **horsepower** (hp). A few of them are more like racing cars that have been redesigned for use on public roads. The most powerful sports cars are often called muscle cars. The most expensive are called supercars. Supercars are so expensive because they use the best materials and technology. There are no sharp divisions between these different types of high-performance cars. A powerful supercar might also be a muscle car.

SUPER CAR

The Ferrari F50 is one of the fastest, most powerful and most expensive cars in the world. It is almost a race car for the road. Its engine was developed from a **Formula 1** race-car engine. Inside, it is quite bare, just like a race car. The F50 is a very high-performance sports car for super-rich drivers.

COBRA POWER

One of the most famous sports cars was created by an American ex-race car driver. Carroll Shelby redesigned a British sports car, the AC Ace, and created the AC Cobra. It was a great road car and was also successful in motor racing. Its 4.7-liter **V8** engine gave it a top speed of up to 140 mph (225 km/hr). Later versions had larger engines up to seven liters, giving them a top speed of 165 mph (265 km/hr). The Cobra was so successful that replicas, or copies, of them can still be bought in kit form for people to build themselves.

FUN ON WHEELS

The German BMW Z3 is a typical modern sports car. It's a great-looking, open-top two-seater. It can be powered by a range of different engines to suit the performance that different drivers want.

BMW Z3

Engine size: 3.0-l **inline** 6
Engine power: 230 hp
Length: 13 ft, 4 in. (4.05 m)
Weight: 3,000 lb (1,360 kg)
Top speed: 150 mph (240 km/hr)
Seats: 2

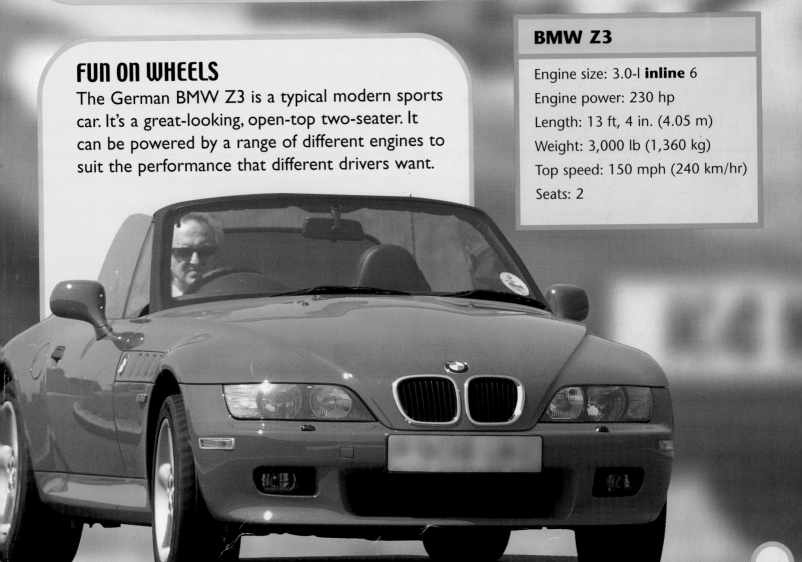

DESIGN FOR SPORTS

A sports car's size, shape, weight, and engine power are chosen by its designer to give the car the smooth, outstanding **performance** that sports cars are known for.

The size and shape of a sports car are very important. A small, lightweight car is more **maneuverable** than a big, heavy car. So, most sports cars are built to be small and light. There is often room inside for only a driver and one passenger. A sports car also has to be the right shape to slip through the air quickly. That is why most sports cars have a low-slung body sitting close to the ground. It has to look sporty and exciting, too. A smooth, gently curving body looks good and also lets air slide easily over the car. In many ways, the car's shape and design is decided by the performance it has to deliver.

BEST-SELLER

The Mazda MX-5 is the world's best-selling sports car. It has the layout of a classic sports car. It is a small, open-top two-seater. It has an engine mounted at the front of the car, which drives the rear wheels. All sports cars used to be built like this, because it is a good way to achieve the performance and handling necessary for a sports car.

DRIVING A LIGHTWEIGHT

The Lotus Elise can go faster and run better than many sports cars with bigger, more powerful engines. The reason for this is that the car is very light in weight. Its **chassis,** or frame, is made from **aluminum,** and its body is made from a material called **fiberglass.** The whole car weighs only 1,655 pounds (755 kg). That's about half the weight of many high-performance cars. Its lightness means that it can perform like a race car using a smaller 1.8-liter, 122-**horsepower** engine.

OPEN TO THE AIR

Even more fun than a sports car is a convertible sports car. Some sports cars have a fixed metal roof that can't be removed. Some have a detachable (easily taken off) solid roof. Others have a roof made from soft material that folds away behind the seats. The Mercedes-Benz SLK is different. It has a solid roof that can fold like a soft roof at the flick of a switch. Within 30 seconds, the trunk opens, the roof and rear window fold back out of sight, and the trunk closes again.

Mercedes-Benz SLK 32 AMG

Engine size: 3.2-l **V6**
Engine power: 354 hp
Length: 13 ft (4 m)
Weight: 3,295 lb (1,495 kg)
Top speed: 155 mph (250 km/hr)
Seats: 2

TRACK CARS

The designers who create racing sports cars use every trick of technology and materials available to produce the fastest cars.

They often make use of parts and materials developed for other vehicles. For example, the **disc brakes** that stop race cars were originally developed for aircraft. Eventually, new technology that proves its worth on the racetrack is built into new road-going sports cars. Racing sports cars are lighter, more powerful, and more **streamlined** than road-going sports cars. Racing sports cars also need an extra-strong **chassis,** or frame, to stand up to super-fast cornering without bending or twisting. To make the car lighter, some of the parts that are usually made from steel are replaced by parts made from lighter materials. **Aluminum** and **carbon fiber** are often chosen.

DAY AND NIGHT AT THE WHEEL

Most motor races last up to about three hours, but the world-famous Le Mans sports car race lasts for 24 hours. Each of the specially designed cars is driven by a team of drivers who each take turns at the wheel. The fastest Le Mans sports cars can reach 220 mph (350 km/hr) on the fastest parts of the French racing circuit.

Chrysler Le Mans racing sports car

Engine size: 6.0-l **V8**
Engine power: 585 **hp**
Length: 15 ft, 3 in. (4.65 m)
Weight: 2,000 lb (900 kg)
Top speed: 220 mph (350 km/hr)
Seats: 1

CARS WITH A SPOILER

Racing sports cars often have a winglike strip called a **spoiler** at the back. The spoiler helps increase the car's grip on the road. As the spoiler cuts through the air, it pushes the car downward. The faster the car goes, the more downward force the spoiler produces, pushing the car down more and more. This helps the car take turns faster, because the tires grip better.

spoiler

SPEEDY REPAIRS

Racing sports cars are designed to be taken apart very quickly. They may need to have damaged parts replaced. The car's nose and tail are usually detachable so that new ones can be put on in a few seconds. During a long race, a car will probably also need to have its tires replaced at least once. This is done by changing the whole wheel. Each wheel on a road car is held in place by four or five nuts and bolts. A racing sports car's wheels are usually held on by one big nut. A power tool is used to spin it off. This way, the wheel can be taken off and replaced in a couple of seconds.

This Porsche 911 GT1-98 is having its wheels changed during a pit stop.

MCLAREN F1
THE DESIGN FORMULA

The McLaren F1 is the world's most advanced sports car. It was designed by the same team that produces McLaren **Formula 1** race cars.

The aim was to design the ultimate sports car using methods and materials from Formula 1 racing. The McLaren F1 can accelerate as fast as a race car and reach a top speed of 240 mph (386 km/hr). Every detail of the car was designed to be the best possible weight, strength, and shape. Designers made the car as light as possible because lightweight cars **accelerate** faster than heavy cars and generally handle better. Another way to boost acceleration is to use a more powerful engine. The F1 is powered by a 600-**horsepower** engine made specially for the F1 by BMW Motorsport. The shape of a sports car's body is also very important. The wrong shape can slow the car down. The F1's body is designed to let air flow around it as smoothly as possible.

POWER PLANT

The McLaren F1's engine is a 6.1-liter **V12** built with racing engine know-how. It's the smallest and lightest V12 ever built for a **production car**. It's about six times more powerful than the engine of a family car of the same weight. The main part of the engine, called the engine block, is made from **aluminum** instead of steel to make the car lighter.

The McLaren F1 engine (left) is controlled by a computer ten times more powerful than the computers used in most family cars.

STAYING ON THE LEVEL

When an F1 driver brakes, the **spoiler** at the back of the car tilts up. Air rushing over the top of the car hits the spoiler and pushes the back of the car downward. This downward force gives the rear wheels more grip so that they can slow the car down without skidding. The spoiler also helps to stop something called diving. Most cars dip, or dive, at the front when they brake hard. The F1's spoiler pushes the back end of the car down, keeping the car level.

TUNNEL TESTS

The shape of the McLaren F1 was tested in a **wind tunnel.** As air was blown through the tunnel, the air pressure was measured at many points all over the car's body. To give an even better picture of how air flowed over the car, it was given a thick coat of paint that glows in the dark. The blowing air made the wet paint run and spread. The paint moved farthest where the air flowed fastest.

The McLaren F1's doors are designed to open upward and outward.

MCLAREN F1
HAND-BUILT WITH CARBON FIBER

Sports cars are usually made mostly from steel, but there are other materials that are lighter and stronger than steel. One example is **carbon fiber.**

Most of the McLaren F1 is made from carbon fiber. In fact, the McLaren F1 is the world's first all-carbon-fiber road car. Most sports cars are mass-produced. This means that they are built in large numbers on production lines. Fewer McLaren F1s were built, and each car was built by hand. When construction was complete, the car's body was painted with a special water-based paint. This paint is kinder to the environment than the oil-based paints used on most cars. The car has two onboard computers. One controls the engine to make sure it always works at peak **performance.** The second computer controls all the other electronic systems. It even knows when the car is doing more than 130 mph (210 km/hr) and locks the windows so they can't be opened.

A METAL OVERCOAT
The McLaren F1's windshield is covered by a metal coating so thin that it is see-through. This metallic film tints the screen, but it is not there to look pretty. It is designed to do an important job. An electric current passes through the metal layer, heating it up and gently warming the glass windshield. The warmth keeps the windshield free of mist and perfectly clear.

WHEEL DEALS

The McLaren F1's rear tires are bigger than its front tires. Most road cars have wheels and tires that are all the same size. **Formula 1** race cars have bigger rear tires. This is because the rear wheels are driven by the engine. Big, wide tires grip the ground better than small, thin tires, so the car can **accelerate** without skidding. The McLaren F1 has bigger rear tires for the same reason.

DUAL PURPOSE

Exhaust gases leave the engine through four big tubes called mufflers. Their main job is to make the engine quieter. But the designers have cleverly given them a second job that makes the car safer. In an accident, the mufflers take some of the force of the crash. This helps to protect the people in the passenger compartment.

silencers

MCLAREN F1
SIMPLY FAST

The McLaren F1 can perform better than any other car on the road. Its combination of **acceleration,** speed, and **road-holding** are unmatched even by some race cars.

From a standing start, the McLaren F1 can reach 60 mph (100 km/hr) in just over three seconds. A typical family car would take about ten seconds to reach the same speed. By then, the F1 could be doing more than 125 mph (200 km/hr). This is about as fast as most family cars can go, but the F1 can keep on accelerating. About 30 seconds after starting, it can hit its top speed of 240 mph (386 km/hr). That's about the same as the top speed of a **Formula 1** race car and almost as fast as a U.S. Champ car, the world's fastest **circuit race** car!

F1 VERSUS F1
Amazingly, test drives have shown that the McLaren F1 can actually accelerate faster than a Formula 1 race car from 150 mph (240 km/hr) to 170 mph (270 km/hr). Its designers were able to give it such great **performance** because they didn't have to stick to any of the rules that the designers of Formula 1 race cars have to follow.

DRIVER OR PILOT?

The McLaren F1's seats are set in a unique way. Most sports cars have two seats, side by side. The McLaren F1's driver sits in the middle of the car, like a fighter pilot or the driver of a single-seat race car. The seat is molded to the driver's body, just like the seat of a Formula 1 race car. Two seats are side by side behind the driver's seat.

LIGHT WORK

Saving weight was so important to the McLaren F1's performance that every part was specially designed to save a few more pounds. Even its stereo is half the weight of a normal car stereo. The tools supplied with most cars are usually made from steel, but the McLaren F1's toolkit is made from a lighter metal called **titanium** to save more weight.

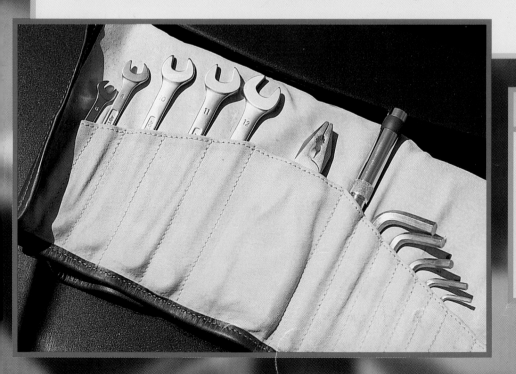

McLaren F1

Engine size: 6.1-l **V12**
Engine power: 627 **hp**
Length: 14 ft (4.3 m)
Weight: 2,510 lb (1,140 kg)
Top speed: 240 mph (386 km/hr)
Seats: 3

ENGINE POWER

Sports cars are powered by the same type of engines as most family cars. All engines are designed to release energy from fuel. The energy is used to turn the car's wheels. However, sports car engines usually have higher **performance.**

Sports car engines have from four to twelve **cylinders.** Each cylinder is a tube with a close-fitting **piston** that slides up and down inside it. **Fuel** is sprayed into each cylinder one at a time, pressed by the piston, and **ignited** by an electric spark. The burning fuel produces hot gases that expand and push the piston back down the cylinder. The up-and-down movements of all the pistons are changed into a spinning motion that powers the car's wheels. Bigger cylinders hold more fuel and air, so a big engine is usually more powerful than a small engine. But bigger engines are also heavier. To keep a sports car light, its designers usually fit it with a small engine. However, the engine can't be too small or it will lack the necessary power. The designer has to balance power against weight to get the required performance.

The inline 4 engine in a Toyota MR2.

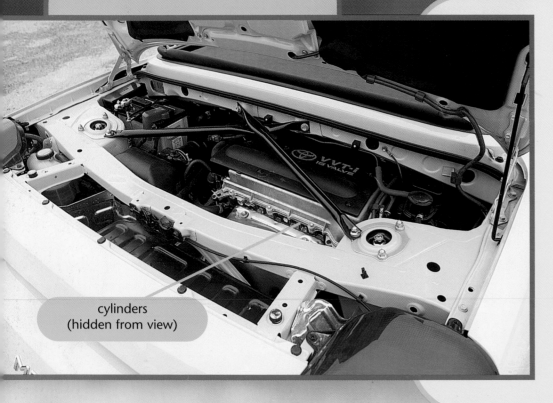

cylinders
(hidden from view)

LINES AND VEES

The Toyota MR2 sports car is powered by a four-cylinder engine. The cylinders stand upright in a row. It is called an **inline engine.** If a sports car designer wants to use a bigger engine with more than six cylinders, there is not enough room to fit them in one long row. One answer is to have two rows, side by side. Usually, the two rows are arranged in a V shape. The eight-cylinder **V8** is a popular sports car engine.

FLAT ENGINES

The Porsche Boxster uses another type of engine, called a flat 6. Its cylinders neither stand upright nor lean over to make a V shape. They lie flat. Imagine three bottles lying side by side. Now add a second row of three bottles bottom-to-bottom with the first row. That's how the cylinders are laid out in a flat 6 engine. With the cylinders lying flat, the weight of the engine is carried low, making the car more stable.

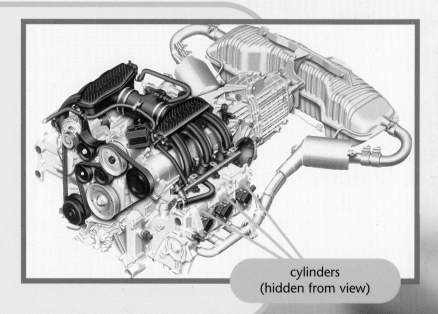

cylinders
(hidden from view)

This illustration shows the combination of toothed wheels and shafts used to produce first and fourth gears.

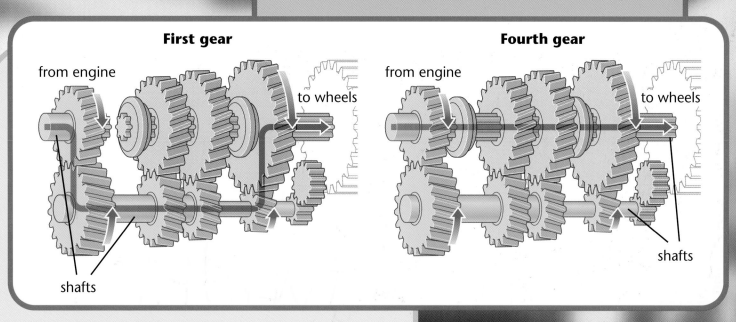

First gear

from engine

to wheels

shafts

Fourth gear

from engine

to wheels

shafts

A BOX OF TEETH

A sports car engine turns a set of toothed wheels in the **transmission. Shafts** connect the transmission to the car's wheels. The driver chooses which **gear** to use. By changing gear, the driver can make the engine drive the car's wheels at anything from walking speed to its top speed.

Porsche Boxster S

Engine size: 3.2-l flat 6
Engine power: 260 **hp**
Length: 14 ft (4.32 m)
Weight: 2,885 lb (1,295 kg)
Top speed: 164 mph (264 km/hr)
Seats: 2

MUSCLE CARS

Some high-**performance** cars owe their **acceleration** and speed to a huge engine under the hood.

The smallest road cars have an engine less than one liter in size. That's smaller than some motorcycle engines! An engine this size produces as little as 50 **horsepower.** A small sports car is driven by an engine roughly twice this size and power. A **Formula 1** race car is powered by a 3-liter engine. But muscle cars are powered by engines of five liters or more, sometimes a lot more. These big-engine chargers include the Chevrolet Corvette and Ford Mustang, but the classic muscle car is the Chrysler Viper. Its driver sits behind a massive 8-liter, 450-horsepower engine. No wonder the car has such a long hood!

AMERICA'S WILD HORSE

The Ford Mustang is one of the most famous cars in the U.S. and also the country's best-selling muscle car. It was designed in the early 1960s to offer young drivers more excitement behind the wheel. Since then, it has been redesigned and updated year after year. Today, with a 4.6-liter **V8** engine growling under the hood, the Mustang can go 60 mph (100 km/hr) in less than five seconds and reach a top speed of more than 155 mph (250 km/hr).

The Viper GTS/R prototype on display in January 2000.

HIGHWAY SNAKE

The Dodge Viper started life as a a type of car called a concept car. Concept cars show what designers think future cars might look like. Many of them are never made for sale, but so many people liked the Viper that Chrysler decided to build it. Its huge engine was developed from a truck engine. Its body was carefully designed to look good and also to remain stable at high speeds.

Chrysler Viper

Engine size: 8.0-l V10

Engine power: 450 hp

Length: 14 ft, 9 in (4.5 m)

Weight: 3,500 lb (1,590 kg)

Top speed: 192 mph (309 km/hr)

Seats: 2

The original Chevrolet Corvette was the first U.S. sports car. It went on sale in 1953.

A RUMBLING FAVORITE

The Corvette ZR-1 was a true supercar. Its rumbling 5.7-liter V8 engine soon made it the favorite muscle car of the United States when it went on sale in 1989. The huge 340-horsepower engine can launch the 3,300-pound (1.65 ton) car from 0 to 60 mph (100 km/hr) in only 4.5 seconds.

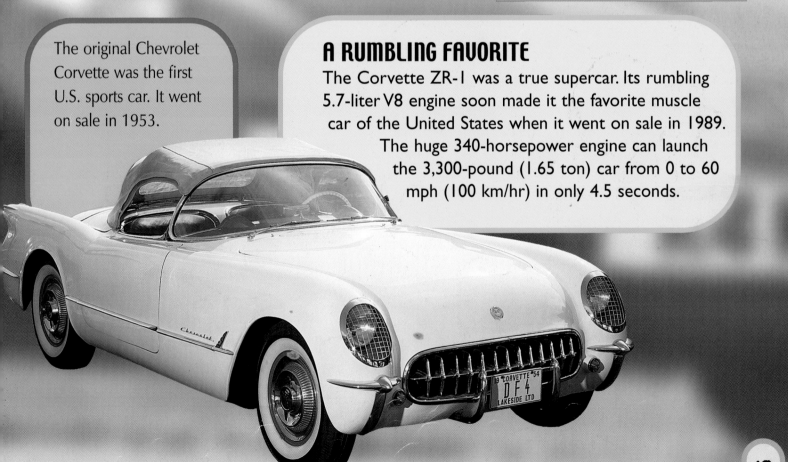

SMOOTH BODIES

The shape of a sports car affects its **acceleration,** top speed, and **handling.** Designing the right shape improves its **performance.**

When a sports car moves, it has to push the air out of the way. Some of the engine's power is wasted in moving against the push of air, called **drag.** Different shapes cause different amounts of drag. A smooth body is better because no parts stick out to catch the air rushing past the car. In some sports cars, the engine is behind the driver. These cars are lower in the front and so produce less drag. However, making the car fun to drive is just as important as giving it a perfect design. A traditional sports car has an engine at the front and an open top. This is not the fastest shape, but it is a lot of fun to drive.

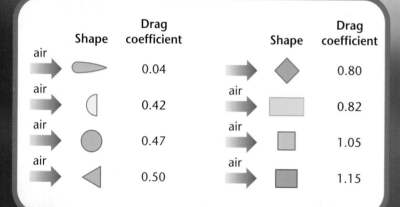

	Shape	Drag coefficient		Shape	Drag coefficient
air		0.04	air		0.80
air		0.42	air		0.82
air		0.47	air		1.05
air		0.50	air		1.15

This diagram shows the different coefficient of drag numbers produced by different shapes. The shapes with the smallest number give the least amount of drag.

WHAT A DRAG

The most **streamlined** sports cars are designed to create the least drag. The shape of the car is tested to find out how easily it moves through the air. The tests result in a number that shows how slippery the car is. This number is called the coefficient of drag. The smaller the number, the more slippery the car is. For a car the shape of a brick, the number is 1.0 or more. For a boxy family car, it is about 0.38. For very streamlined cars, like the Ferrari Enzo (below), it is 0.30 or less.

COOL BODIES

A car's body must have holes in it. The engine needs air to burn its fuel and for cooling. If the body were completely closed, the engine would be starved of air. This would cause it to overheat and break down. The air enters the body through holes called ducts. They are carefully designed to let in the right amount of air without causing a lot of drag.

A Ferrari Testarossa with air intake ducts on the sides.

SO SMOOTH

The Lamborghini Murciélago is one of the most streamlined cars ever made. Its headlights sit behind glass covers. Its sideview mirrors are beautifully curved so that air slips around them. Its windows wrap around the car in line with the body. There are no bumps in the bodywork that might slow down the air flowing around the car.

Lamborghini Murciélago

Engine size: 6.2-l **V12**

Engine power: 580 **hp**

Length: 15 ft (4.58 m)

Weight: 3,640 lb (1,650 kg)

Top speed: 205 mph (330 km/hr)

Seats: 2

SUPERCARS

Supercars are the fastest and most expensive high-**performance** road cars. But only the wealthiest drivers can enjoy race car performance on the road.

Sports cars are small and lightweight, but supercars are often heavier. They make up for their extra weight in two ways. First, they have a more powerful engine. Second, they are usually more **streamlined.** In 1985, the designers of the Lamborghini Diablo supercar were asked to produce the world's fastest **production car.** It would have to reach at least 200 mph (320 km/hr) to beat the competition. The designers reduced its weight by using lighter materials. It also had the most powerful engine Lamborghini had ever built. It was indeed the fastest production car. And as we have seen, the designers at McLaren have also built a new type of supercar—the McLaren F1.

LAMBORGHINI DIABLO

The Lamborghini Diablo is an amazing machine. Inside its elegant, swooping body, a huge, roaring 6-liter engine sits behind the driver. The 550-**horsepower** engine can accelerate the 3,530-pound (1,600-kilogram) car to about 205 mph (325 km/hr). **Acceleration** is helped by the fact that most of the body parts, except the roof and the doors, are made from lightweight **carbon fiber.**

Lamborghini Diablo

Engine size: 6.0 l **V12**
Engine power: 550 hp
Length: 14 ft, 7 in (4.47 m)
Weight: 3,580 lb (1,625 kg)
Top speed: 205 mph (325 km/hr)
Seats: 2

JAGUAR XJ220

When the Jaguar XJ220 was designed in 1992, it was to be powered by Jaguar's 5.3-liter V12 engine. However, before the car was built, this engine was replaced by a special 3.5-liter V6 racing engine. The racing engine was more powerful. It gave the new car a top speed of more than 210 mph (340 km/hr), making it the fastest production car ever built at the time. Jaguar announced that it would make only 350 XJ220s. Within a few days, it had received over 1,200 orders.

FERRARI F40

Ferrari's F40 was designed specially to celebrate the Italian carmaker's 40th anniversary. It was based on an earlier Ferrari, the 288 GTO, which had been developed for motor racing. The F40 was given a much lighter body made from carbon fiber instead of steel. Inside, the car was quite bare, adding to the feeling that it was a road-going race car.

DESIGNING FOR SAFETY

Modern sports cars are designed to be safe. If the worst happens and a sports car is involved in an accident, it must protect the people inside it.

When a car hits something, it stops incredibly suddenly. People's soft bodies are easily injured by the violent forces in a crash. Some of a sports car's safety features are designed so that the passengers come to a halt a little less suddenly. The seats, doors, and **dashboard** are padded. Seatbelts hold the passengers safely in their seats and stop them from being thrown out through the windshield. However, a seatbelt does not hold the head. The head can fly forward, causing neck injuries, or it may hit the steering wheel. To prevent this, most cars now have airbags that inflate in an accident and cushion the head.

FASTEN BELTS

Seat belts usually allow a driver or passenger to move around freely. But when a car hits something, the belt locks and keeps the person wearing it from flying forward. Some sports cars are fitted with an extra safety feature called a pre-tensioner. In a collision, the seat belt doesn't just lock, it actually tightens and pulls the driver or passenger back into the seat.

SAFETY BAGS

When a car hits something, **sensors** detect the sudden stop and trigger the airbags. An **igniter** sets off a gas capsule that blows up the bag like a balloon. All of this happens within a fraction of a second. It has to be that quick to catch the driver's head before it hits the steering wheel.

ROCK AND ROLL

Convertible sports cars often have a roll bar. A roll bar is a thick bar that curves up behind the seats, above the driver's head. The roll bar has a life-saving purpose. If the car turns over, the roll bar supports the weight of the car and stops it from crushing the passengers underneath. Some cars that seem to have no roll bar have a very strong windshield frame that does the same job.

The Ferarri 360 Spider has an individual roll bar for each seat.

CRASH TEST DUMMIES

All new car designs are tested by deliberately crashing them to make sure that they meet international safety regulations. Inside the car are life-size dummies designed to resemble a human driver and passengers. They weigh the same as people and they have joints in all the right places. They are also fitted with instruments to record the forces that act on them during a crash.

FUN CARS

A handful of sports cars are designed to be totally impractical for anything but having fun. They're designed and built for drivers to enjoy driving. Most of them look very basic indeed. They seem little more than an engine, a seat, and four wheels. Because they are so basic, they are also amazingly light.

The tiny Caterham 7, for example, is more powerful than the 3.8-liter Ford Mustang muscle car, but is less than one-third the weight of the mighty Mustang. This combination of more power and less weight produces amazingly fast **acceleration**, sharper turning and higher speeds. The fastest Caterham 7 model, the Superlight R500, can go from 0 to 60 mph (100 km/hr) in 3.4 seconds, compared to 9.3 seconds for the Mustang.

CATERHAM 7

The Caterham 7 gives drivers a thrilling and exciting ride. It's an open-top, ultra-lightweight car. There are several different models powered by different engines. Some of them even use engines from high-performance motorcycles. The cars weigh about 1,100 pounds (500 kilograms). That's less than one third of the weight of a Ford Mustang.

Caterham 7 Superlight R500

Engine size: 1.8-l **inline** 4
Engine power: 230 **hp**
Length: 11 ft (3.38 m)
Weight: 1,000 lb (460 kg)
Top speed: 150 mph (240 km/hr)
Seats: 2

ON THE PROWL

The Chrysler Prowler is designed to look dramatic and make people stop and stare. Its styling was inspired by cars called hot rods, fast cars built by car lovers. Some hot rods are built for racing. Others are built for show. They are often built to look like old-fashioned family cars, but under their outer bodies they have a very powerful engine. The interior often has leather seats and a super sound system. The fun shape and extra weight of the stereo, special interior, and other additions, however, affect the car's **performance.**

The designer of the Chrysler Prowler had to balance appearance against performance, **handling,** and speed.

ATOM POWER

The British Ariel Atom looks like a metal skeleton on wheels. It has no doors, no windshield, and no roof. There is nowhere to store luggage. It certainly isn't **streamlined** either. And yet it is very fast. Its top speed is 155 mph (250 km/hr). Its secret is that it is a whopping 342 pounds (155 kilograms) lighter than the ultra-light Lotus Elise sports car and has 60 more horsepower than the Elise.

Every sports car is designed with a particular type of driver in mind. This table compares the basic specifications of some of today's best-known sports cars.

Car	Engine	Weight (lb / kg)	Top speed (mph/ km/hr)	Time (seconds) 0–60 mph (0–100 km/hr)
Ariel Atom 190	1.8-liter **inline** 4	1,300 / 600	155 / 250	unknown
BMW Z3	3.0-liter inline 6	3,000 / 1,360	150 / 240	6.0
Chevrolet Corvette	5.7-liter **V8**	3,200 / 1,455	175 / 280	4.5
Chrysler Prowler	3.5-liter V6	2,850 / 1,295	130 / 210	6.5
Chrysler Viper	8.0-liter V10	3,500 / 1,590	192 / 309	4.5
Ferrari Enzo	6.0-liter V12	3,020 / 1,370	220 / 350	3.7
Ferrari F50	4.7-liter V12	2,710 / 1,230	200 / 320	3.7
Ford Mustang	4.6-liter V8	3,664 / 1,662	155 / 250	4.5
Jaguar XJ220	3.5-liter V6	3,031 / 1,375	220 / 350	3.8
Lamborghini Diablo	6.0-liter V12	3,580 / 1,625	205 / 325	3.8
Lotus 340R	1.8-liter inline 4	1,488 / 675	130 / 210	4.6
Lotus Elise	1.8-liter inline 4	1,665 / 755	125 / 200	5.7
Mazda MX-5	1.8-liter inline 4	2,350 / 1,065	130 / 205	8.4
McLaren F1	6.1-liter V12	2,510 / 1,140	240 / 386	3.2
Mercedes-Benz SLK 32 AMG	3.2-liter V6	3,330 / 1,495	155 / 250	5.2
Porsche 911 GT3	3.6-liter flat 6	2,980 / 1,350	185 / 300	4.8
Porsche Boxster	3.2-liter flat 6	2,850 / 1,295	164 / 264	5.9
Toyota MR2	1.8-liter inline 4	2,120 / 960	130 / 210	7.9

JAGUAR'S E-TYPE

In the 1960s, one of the most famous sports cars in the world was the Jaguar E-type. Originally, the E-type was designed as a race car. However, when Jaguar pulled out of motor racing, the E-type was redesigned as a road car. A 1961 model with a 3.8-liter engine could reach 150 mph (240 km/hr).

FURTHER READING

Chelsea House Publishing Staff. *Modern Sports Cars.* Broomall, Penn.: Chelsea House Publishers, 1997.

McKenna, A. T. *Corvette.* Edina, Minn.: ABDO Publishing Company, 2000.

McKenna, A. T. *Lamborghini.* Edina, Minn.: ABDO Publishing Company, 2000.

Wright, David. *The Story of Porsches.* Milwaukee, Wisc.: Gareth Stevens Incorporated, 2002.

FERRARI'S REDHEAD

Sports cars became very popular in the 1950s. Ferrari built one of its most famous sports cars, the Testarossa, in 1956. It was called Testarossa (Italian for redhead) after the red covers on top of the engine. It was a racing sports car and it was very successful. Its 300-**horsepower**, 3-liter **V12** engine and lightweight **alloy** body gave it a top speed of about 170 mph (270 km/hr).

GLOSSARY

accelerate go faster. A driver accelerates by pressing the accelerator pedal.

alloy metal made from a mixture of two or more different metals

aluminum lightweight metal that is easy to bend and shape

carbon fiber strong and lightweight material made from strands of carbon embedded in hard plastic

chassis frame on which a vehicle is built

circuit racing motor racing around a specially-built racetrack

cylinder tube-shaped part of a car engine where the fuel is burned. A sports car may have between four and twelve cylinders.

dashboard panel in a car in which the driver's instruments are located

disc brakes brakes made of a disc (attached to a vehicle's wheel) between two tough pads. The disc spins with the wheel. When the driver presses the brake pedal, the pads grip the disc and slow it down.

drag force of air on a car that slows the car down. Drag is also called air resistance.

exhaust gases that rush out of an engine after fuel has been burned

fiberglass strong, lightweight material made from glass fibers mixed with plastic. Some sports cars have a fiberglass body because fiberglass is lighter than metal.

Formula 1 leading international motor racing championship

fuel substance that is burned to produce power. Sports cars' engines burn gasoline, a liquid made from oil.

gear a wheel with teeth around its edge. When two gear wheels are put together so that their teeth interlock, turning one wheel makes the other wheel turn, too. If the wheels are the same size, they turn at the same speed.

handling way a car responds or reacts when it is being driven

horsepower (hp) unit of measurement of the power of an engine, equal to the power to lift 550 pounds one foot in one second, or 746 watts of electrical power

ignite set on fire. The fuel inside an engine is ignited by an electric spark.

inline engine type of engine that has the engine's cylinders arranged in a line in a single bank

maneuverable steerable. A more maneuverable car can make tighter turns than most other cars.

performance how well a car works overall. A high-performance car is capable of faster acceleration and higher speeds than most cars.

piston part of a car's engine that slides back and forth inside the cylinder, where the fuel is burned. The back and forth movements turn the car's wheels.

production car car built in large numbers for sale

road-holding car's ability to grip the road without skidding, especially as it turns corners

sensors devices that take measurements. Sensors measure everything from engine temperature to oil pressure. They are connected to the instruments in front of the driver and to the car's computer, if it has one.

shaft revolving rod. Shafts are used in cars to transmit motion or power from one place to another.

spoiler a panel or strip fitted to a car to produce a downward force or stop the car from taking off like a plane when it goes very fast

streamlined word used to describe a slim, smooth shape that moves through the air very easily

titanium strong, lightweight metal that is used instead of steel to make some car parts. Titanium is good because it does not rust, and it can withstand very high temperatures.

transmission set of gear wheels of different sizes. By linking different gear wheels so that their teeth lock together, the engine can be made to turn the car's wheels at a much wider range of speeds. Selecting different gear wheels like this is also called shifting gear.

V6, V8, V10, V12 type of car engine with six, eight, ten, or twelve cylinders. The cylinders are arranged in two rows, or banks. The two rows of cylinders spin a shaft that runs along the bottom of the engine. The cylinders lean outward from this shaft, giving the engine its V shape. The number after the *V* shows how many cylinders the engine has.

wind tunnel large tube or passage through which air is blown. Models of sports cars and full-size sports cars are tested by placing them in a wind tunnel and studying how air flows around them.

INDEX